SPITTIN' LYRICS N WAXIN' POETIC

First edition. August 17, 2015.

Copyright © 2015 Kevin Alberto Sabio.

ISBN: 979-8223562375

Written by Kevin Alberto Sabio.

DEDICATION

Dedicated to all of those that have something to say, and cannot keep it contained inside. To all of those that have ever spit a verse, waxed poetic, or just shouted at the top of their lungs. Words can be very powerful, and very influential. May you hear what I have to say, and appreciate what I'm saying.

ACKNOWLEDGMENTS

I am not a poet. I have been known to spit some verses over the years, and wax poetic to certain women that I've been interested in dating. But, I repeat...I am *not* a poet. A poet (to me) is someone who lives poetry, who feels the need to spit poetry, to be able to truly express themselves poetically. I *do* like poetry, but it is not my passion.

Having said that...I have had the honor of meeting many poets in my travels. They have been the inspiration for my interest in writing (and sometimes, performing) poetry. I have a number of works that I have kept in the archives, never having shown, nor performed these pieces before. It is because I've had the honor of crossing paths with these people that this project is even possible. Without meeting them, this literary project wouldn't even be considered. These pieces would still be collecting dust in one of my folders, both physical and digital, never to see the light of day. So, it is because of these people, these influencers, these grand wordsmiths, those emcees & dope spitters...that this project is now a reality.

Shout out to my peoples Christopher "Chilo" Cajigas, Mercy Tullis-Bukhari, David "El David" Rodriguez, Katalina Rodriguez, Maria Aponte, Carmen Bardeguez-Brown, Custodio Gomes, Carlos Semanxant, Manuel Melendez, Peggy Robles-Alvarado, Stan "Substantial" Robinson, Afi Makalani, Be One, Al Walker, Jamil "Skript" Jasey, Serena Wills, Sabrina Gilbert, Vladimir "Vitamin V" Rodriguez, Not4Prophet, Oveous Maximus, Mariposa Fernandez, Caridad "La Bruja" De La Luz, and so many others that I can't name.

Table of Contents

Part I: **Heart of a Souljahr**
Internal Conflict
Deaf, Dumb and Blind
I Wonder II: Wordz of Wisdom
Warrior's Call
Untitled Shout
Headache
I Hate His Guts
Pretty Women
Hard Hearted
Chocolate Sprinkles
Culture Clash [Music]
Acts of Honor [Rap Song]
Lawz Unda Da Gun [Rap Song]
For The Censors [Rap Song]
Phunkee Honduran's Flow [Rap Song]

Part II: **Heart of a Lover**
To My Queen (My Dearest Monica)
My Fantasy
What Would It Be Like...?
A Jewel In My Life (I & II)
Love Letter
Courtship
An Ode to Lisa
Adwoa (I, II, & III)
Sonia's Song
Smiley
Lust
Letter From My Heart
The Art of Loving You

KEVIN ALBERTO SABIO

About Last Night
Bonding With You
More Than A Crush
So Open
Lifted Spirits
To My Dearest Yana
The Depths of My Heart
Unrestricted

PART I:
HEART OF A
SOULJAHR

INTERNAL CONFLICT

Why should I care about the problems that exist...?

Why, oh *why* will my combative spirit *not* leave me be, and let my soul exist in complacent peace...?

Must I be that man...that hard brother, that fights and strives for change, while others sit idly by...?

Why won't my inner spirit allow me to give up...?

Shouldn't *I* be able to become apathetic...?

Why won't my spirit let my disenfranchisement take over, and cease with this fight?

Don't *I* deserve some peace...?

Dual forces conflicting for control over my body and mind,

Striving for control over that ultimate, most coveted prize...my soul...

How come I care, when others don't?

Why should *I* continue to fight, when others won't?

Do others *not* understand what's at stake...?

Or...am *I* the only lost one...?

Am *I* the one that doesn't belong...?

Or...has my time, and way of thinking, passed?

Heaven help us all...

© 2001

DEAF, DUMB, AND BLIND

A cancerous lesion that infests the soul,
    Tearing you apart from top to bottom...
    That cancer of ignorance that takes over your mind and body,
    Nonthinking, unfeeling, having no conscience at all...
    No peripheral vision to see beyond that which is right in front of you,
    Never going beyond that which you were told by others,
    Never thinking for one's self...
    They say that ignorance is bliss...but, is it really...?
    Why hate on a man who wears his hair nappy, natural, and long?
    Why hate on a man who chooses to call his creator, Allah?
    How come I have to support the Israelis, but *not* the Palestinians?
    Is it right that I am called a heathen for not going to Sunday service,
    But yet you go all of the time, but *never* follow any of the sacraments, or the
commandments...?
    Why is it more important to never forget the Jewish Holocaust,
    But yet I *need* to get past, and get over slavery...?
    Life must be kind for the Deaf, Dumb, and Blind...
    Yeah, maybe...but, that's *not* me...
    © 2001

I WONDER II (Wordsz of Wisdom)

Why, oh why...I wonder Why...

Why is it that the only time that we see any representation of the Black student population at any of our major universities, it's only when it's on ESPN, when their sports teams are playing?

I Wonder...

Why is it that...time after time, in city after city,

A Black man/woman is shot down by the Powers-That-Be,

And that the *only* guilty party is the Black man/woman him/herself...?

I Wonder...

Why, oh why do the local politicians *always* find the money to build skyscrapers and stadiums,

But can only offer students portable classrooms, and empty promises?

I Wonder...

Why, oh why are my brothers more interested in being ignorant ass niggas from the ghetto,

Instead of being strong, intelligent, Black men?

I Wonder...

Why is it that my people *always* talk about the need of spiritual faith,

But it's always *their* particular faith that they want you to follow?

I Wonder...

Will we ever stop fighting amongst ourselves,

And finally unite against our common foe(s), and their system of oppression?

I Wonder...

When I die, with my warriors spirit,

Will I truly be able to rest in peace?

I Wonder...

© 2001

WARRIOR'S CALL

A daily call to battle to save the masses from the effects of ignorance that plagues their mind, body, and soul,

Though, many times...my services are met with utter resistance...

My ways are not understood, they cast me off as crazy,

They say that I am too angry, and for no reason,

But alas, I keep fighting...

Learning all that I can, so that I can reach that other man,

And somehow hope to make him to understand,

I'm doing this for *you*, brother...

To free you from these limitations and shackles that they've put on your mind, and on our kind,

Trying to keep us ignorant, and lagging far behind...

You're worth *more* than that, man...

The whole good hair/bad hair, light skin/dark skin, rural south/ghetto north,

East coast/West coast, integration/separatist, scrubs/pigeons, chickenhead vs hoodrats...

Man...It's ALL bullshit!!!

They're just trying to mess with your mind, slaughtering our own kind,

Working you to the grind, as they rob you blind...

It's all a game plan...

Making you lose your focus, and forget what to value,

Leaving your history to be a mystery,

As you are left to exist in mental and emotional misery...

...And *that* is why I fight the way that I do!

That, is my calling...

© 2001

UNTITLED SHOUT

Hear me!

What happened to my people?! Where is our pride?

When did it happen that the soul of my Black people died?!

People are now acting crazy, committing deeds that are heinous and bizarre,

How could we have let ourselves descend down so far?

Hateful female gold diggers, misogynistic brothers full of hate and criminality,

Since when did all of this evilness become our main, dominant personality?

Heeding many false prophets, all of them media creations at large,

All of them just out to be Double-HNICs, Head House Niggas In Charge...

They're not here to make a difference, it's only all about self gain,

While the masses continue to suffer, and endure with the pain...

Subversive forces meant to temper our ebb and flow,

Doing nothing for the community, just another dress and pony show...

Silencing our voices, looking to get some stupid ass vote,

When we really need to be organizing and mobilizing, putting our foot on somebody's throat...

Stop it with all of the damn marches, and start cracking somebody's head,

How many times do we have to see our people murdered by the cops, shot down dead?

Learn from our formations in the past, the resistance that they gave,

How they instilled fear but respect from our enemies, how proudly they stood brave...

We need to reestablish our culture, getting back to having cultural pride,

Change our attitude, and make a game plan, or else our people will never survive...

Building our own institutions, truly representing for our people,

No need for government handouts or oppressive police, we can communally be equal...

Absorb the works of our warrior scholars, both from the present, and from the past,

And our former organizational formations, who had already lighted the path...

Following their blueprints and guidelines, make modern amendments when need be,

And then...*only* then, will our people be free...

Uhuru sase

© 2005

HEADACHE

My head hurts...

I get infuriated by reading these opinion pieces in mainstream periodicals,

Some House Nigga, award winning 'journalist' blasting radical black people,

Kissing up to massa, making it seem like everyday Black life under his yoke is all good,

Critical of all radicals, and the Black masses all together...

Must be a sale, cause there's a *whole* lot of selling out going on...

Why is there silence amongst the masses, though? Do they not care...?

Are they not aware of this character assassination from one of our own?

Then again...if they can kill off their own, then they're *not* really one of us...

They are no better than the gangstas, and drug dealers conflicting for turf,

Except, that *their* weapons are a laptop, and a column in massa's paper...

Their words and ignorance make me angry,

But what makes me angrier still...is the silence...

Why do I care so much? Do I have too much time on my hands to think?

But also, can those "journalists" really be that stupid and naïve?

The tension continues to swell upon my dome, adding pressure,

The more I think about it, the more pain I feel, continually reading and hearing their asinine journalism,

Yet, I continue to see apathy and ignorance amongst the masses on the streets...

How do I make the pain stop?

Will it ever go away...?

They blame us for the plights that we endure, claiming that our cries are illegitimate,

"Just pick yourselves up by your bootstraps. I did...look at me"!

The height of their hypocrisy, arrogance, and utter bullshit amazes me...

Come to the neighborhood, Mr/Mrs. Oreo Journalist; it *ain't* all good!

We didn't bring in the drugs, or make the guns; we don't own any breweries...

We didn't make our own poverty, or damage the educational system...

Do we have our issues..? Yes.

Are there issues in our community that we can fix...? Yes, there are a few...

BUT...you sir/madam, are a crab...

You spout off inaccuracies worse than any Euro bigot,

You spread misinformation, biased opinions, and utter lies...

You do this all in the face of those who *created* this situation faced by our community,

...And yet, there is still silence.

I am but one voice...will I be heard?

Or...will I be told to 'calm down', and take it easy?

My head hurts again...

© 2002

I HATE HIS GUTS

May my soul rest in peace, and my head cease aching,
For there are these troublesome thoughts that infest me...
Extreme animosity, and murderous thoughts haunt my vessel,
Thoughts that could sentence me to untold damnation...
The sin, is that of the erasure of the life of my own kin,
The flesh of my flesh, the blood of my blood; he who I am related to...
I despise his bullying ways, his lack of responsibility, his arrogance, his selfish ass,
He who cries 'woe is me', yet is responsible for every woe that he has wrought...
You made your bed, you dumb motherfucker...now *lie* in it!
He, who bullies the seeds of his loins, and batters their carrier about,
His violence goes unchecked, almost as if condoned...
My hatred for my kin grows tirelessly after every act, as he yet stands uninterrupted,
ALWAYS blaming his targets for his actions...
NEVER accepting fault, forever the victim...
...What BULLSHIT!
Thoughts of asphyxiation by my hand, or my belt, or at least an extreme battering,
Assault with a deadly weapon, until my kin moves no more...
Is this normal?
My frustration grows, as the rest of my kin stands idly by,
See no evil, hear no evil, speak no evil...all because he is kin,
I interfere...and yet *I'm* the one that get scolded and reprimanded...
Fuck it...he needs to stop!
But to stop him, will it cost me my sanity, my peace of mind?
Will it cost me my freedom?
This needs to stop..but how?
And yet...He continues on, for a SECOND time,
A new carrier this time, but the same old tactics,
Still battering the seeds of his loins, and their carrier,

Arrogantly, walking around like his shit don't stink,
I still interfere, and yet STILL get reprimanded,
But yet HE is still allowed to continue on...
Truly, I hate his guts...
© 2002, 2015

PRETTY WOMEN

Pretty women on this campus pass me by,
But they wear ill grills, looking all mean, and I wonder why...?
Your physical form instills in me visions of sweet, sensual lovemaking,
But it's that hostile attitude of yours that I really be hating...
Don't you know that your beauty is more than just skin deep...?
You rarely say hello, sporting an attitudinal glare,
Let me holla at you sister...do you have a second to spare...?
Who turned you off, so? Why are you so mad?
Is life dealing with men on this campus *really* that bad...?
I never tried to hurt you, I just wanted to say hello...
Why assume that when I speak, I just want to take you to bed?
Why can't you think that I just *really* wanted to say hello instead?
No I'm not Mr. Big Shot On Campus, and no, I'm not rich,
All I wanted to do was be nice, and say 'hi', why you acting like a b-...
Ah, ah, ah...but, that would be disrespectful of me.
Respect given, is respect earned...
Always remember sista, that you are a true queen,
That whenever you walk around with your head held high, your presence will always gleam,
Brighten up your face girl, why do you choose to walk around, looking so sour?
Show off your true beauty, your true inner power...
Yes, you are attractive, that don't mean that you should act stank,
Chill out a little, enjoy your life...
Just a little friendly advice, from a brother to a sista,
Just ask yourself...are you pretty *just* on the outside, or from the inside, too?
© 2001

HARD HEARTED

I gave away my heart to you, thinking that it was wanted,
 I wrote you love letters, and my full affections were given to you, undaunted...
 The feelings I had of utmost joy, to have you by my side,
 The way that my emotions swelled, filling with so much pride...
 I cared for you, and you meant a lot to me, though I hadn't known you long,
 For me to feel this way for you...? My heart just *couldn't* be wrong...
 I confided in you, and let down my guard,
 For me to feel safe in your heart...? That wasn't real hard...
 You had told me that you got me, and I'd let you know that you were right,
 'Fore why should I deny the truth, fore your heart you cannot fight...
 I told you what I felt for you, letting you know of my true intentions,
 But because of circumstances on *your* end, my heart is now on suspension...
 I'm feeling hurt, I feel betrayed, my heart's now blue and gloomy,
 I've been so honest, I kept it real...why did you have to delude me...?
 I gave you my heart, soul, and mind...being a sweet true brother,
 But while I was with you, giving you my all...you neglected to mention the
other...
 Well...I hope that you're happy, that he treats you right, that he fills your heart
with glee,
 I shall move on, and I don't hate ya...but the stay THE HELL away from me...
 I won't be mean, I will say 'hi', but that's *all* that it shall be,
 And if anything happens, and it all goes wrong...I'll give you *no* sympathy...
 We can still remain cool, there is no hate, we may even get back to be friends,
 But even if that happens, just to let you know...I'll NEVER trust you again...
 © 2000

CHOCOLATE SPRINKLES
(On Top of This University)

Whence I first came upon this scene, my mood turned very crabby,

To walk across these campus grounds, and see *no* signs of Black solidarity...

Walking on my way to class, my fellow Black students pass me by,

Eye contact is made with very few, and *not one* of them said to me 'hi'...

At first I tried greeting them, but their stank ass kept walking,

Added to the fact that they talk mad trash, my attitude started growing...

Never dealing with each other, just sticking to their own little cliques,

And in a place where we're a true minority, seeing that shit *really* makes me sick..

Sistas dealing with brothers just for status, or materials,

And with brothers here doing the same thing, Black existence here is so trivial...

Shouting out ghettos, bed hopping, smoking weed,

Isn't this supposed to be an institution of higher learning, indeed...?

Oh, I've met a few good, strong souls who have challenged this perception,

But for an overall view, we're headed in a downward direction...

In this vast sea of vanilla, it is really a sad sight to see,

It is how I see these Chocolate Sprinkles on top of this university...

Don't let our 'large' numbers fool you, as if on this campus, there are no problems,

Because if we could come together as one, we would be able to stop them...

As if they have our best interest at heart, putting our educational needs on the shelf,

Walking along these campus grounds, lacking in knowledge of self...

These Black student organizations, going unsupported, all falling to the wayside,

Walking around as if in a fashion show, having no sense of cultural pride...

Start biting into the cone, beyond the surface, getting past the crown,

Only on the surface it is chocolate; it it still very much vanilla on the way down...

We need to learn to come together; and any issues we face, we can stop them,
And if you're not a part of the solution, then your a part of the problem...
Will we ever get there yet...? I don't know, we'll have to see,
And that's just how I see these Chocolate Sprinkles on top of this University...
© 2001

CULTURE CLASH

Verse 1

We live in a world of diversity,
Different cultures and ethnicities,
We live together and all show our pride,
To all of those around...
People of different races live with me,
Together we make this society,
We live together, but there's ignorance...
There's hate, there's violence...and there there's separation...
Of a people, of a skin tone,
Then everybody's fighting (oh, no!)

Chorus:

Conflict rising cause a culture clash
It causes violence, and thinking that's rash
Don't oppress me, and I won't diss you,
If we can't stop fighting, then what'll we do..?

Rap Verse #1:

Livin' in a world where they judge you by your skin,
They givin' you problems, and you know you can't win,
First they gonna diss, then they try to dismiss,
It's a big problem, that you know we gotta fix,
First it's a fight, then you got a big brawl,
Then it starts growing, and it might kill us all,
Don't mind separation, but not extermination,
Thinkin' gets cloudy, and tears apart a whole nation,
We gotta stop the problem, not with actions that are rash,
Then it escalates, and we gotta live with Culture Clash

Chorus: (2X)

Verse 2

Bringing in children of a mix background,

They get teased, and get people that hound,
Programming their thoughts to hate a creed,
We're self destructing our society,
Showing racism, and denying our own,
Gotta stop the trend, and end the chain,
Be whole, or separate (it's one, or the other..it's gotta change)
It's gotta stop, it's gotta end,
So we can go on living (oh yeah!)
<u>Chorus:</u> (2X)
Conflicts rising cause a Culture Clash,
It causes violence, and thinking that's rash,
Don't oppress me, and I won't diss you,
If we can't stop fighting, then what'll we do?
<u>Rap Verse #2:</u>
Listen...
You know the situation, and you're making mixed kids,
Then they go to school, and get condemned for what you did,
Use ya mind before you send them into society,
Cause then they coming back, and then they're askin' why'd you lie to me...
People shouldn't be ignorant, but you can't be stupid,
Racism is a problem that can't be eluded,
You gotta use your mind, can't be a whining fool,
Either stick with your own, or flood the cultural pool,
Ya think ya livin' happy, but you know it won't last,
Now suffer the effects of the Culture Clash...
<u>Chorus:</u> (2X)
Conflicts rising cause a Culture Clash
It's causes violence, and thinking that's rash,
Don't oppress me, and I won't diss you,
If we can't stop fighting, then what'll we do...?
© 1993 Kevin Alberto Sabio
A New Latin Swing Joint

ACTS OF HONOR

<u>**Verse 1**</u>

The other day, my Homie had gotten japped in the face,
(*And, yo*) word is born...you know he felt disgraced,
Caught on the DL, in front of the whole crew,
Ay, yo, son...I was pissed...I didn't know what to do,
We went home pissed, and you know he was hurtin',
I'm plannin' some payback, that kid's final curtain,
I felt like a fool...yo, we shoulda had his back,
But the head of my crew said (*Nah...we can't do that*),
Knew he was wrong, we shoulda fucked up that kid,
We shoulda gotten him real good for the damage that he did,
I'm feelin' low, I felt like a chump,
Cause as soon as it happened, we shoulda been down to jump,
We gotta have payback, I'm plannin' some late hits,
Wanna scare that punk ass so bad, make that Nigga catch mad shit,
Throw a fair one, so that we can see yo skills,
Before we fuck you up, and then go for the kill,
He crossed the line...he should prepare to die,
He used his boy, and then he buss him in the eye,
You ain't safe, kid...you know you're a goner,
You gonna catch wreck, cause I'm fightin' wit the Acts of Honor...

<u>**Verse 2**</u>

I've seen him a few, in school, and in the streets,
That dumb muthafucka's the one we gotta beat,
(*Yeah*) He thinks he's safe, that shit is squashed and dead,
But if I had a gat...I'd cap him in his head,
Acts of Honor, back my boys til the end,
I catch yo ass, and six you will descend,
I gotta bring you down, I'm gonna whip your ass,
Cause it's Law by Honor, one I must surpass,
My hate is intense, reminiscin' makes me mad,
Until money's dead is the only way that I'll be glad,

He needs to suffer, we gotta have fear and pain,
I need to prove my honor, I got nothin' else to gain,
Watch your back, cause I'm gonna hunt you down,
And then I'm gonna herb ya (*yeah...ya fuckin' clown!*)
Gettin' herbed, getting' snuffed for my boy,
To see you in pain, is gonna bring me mad joy,
Go through the ranks, herbing your whole squad,
And then when I get to you, I shoot-the-two to do the job,
Now I'm calm, but yo ass is still a goner,
Reasons defined, I'm fightin' wit the Acts of Honor,

<u>Verse 3</u>

I'm feelin' mad, I'm thinkin' like a criminal,
I want to see him dead, though the damage was minimal,
Go wit my boy, and then throw a fair one,
Or, go on the DL, and get the job quickly done,
Roll wit my troops, herb you in the open,
Buss him lovely, and anyone scopin',
Find him solo, when he's fully exposed,
And then leave him for dead, lettin' his ass decompose,
Step off, money...don't have a death wish,
Or else I'll take a blade to your throat...(*and swish!*)
That's it...so long...peace to ya,
Ya hadda be stupid, and then we hadda herb ya,
Ain't out to diss ya, I just want some payback,
Think about that shit for the next kid you smack,
Don't fight back, just take the punches like a man,
I'll beat you worse than even yo daddy can,
So next time, don't ever think to dishonor,
You gonna catch wreck, cause I'm fightin' wit the Acts of Honor
© 1991-1992

LAWZ UNDA DA GUN

My li'l Homie in the hood is havin' his problems,
    He's not a ruffneck, so find an easy way to solve 'em,
    He's always gettin' his ass kicked by the local dealer,
    My Shorty wants no beef, he's just a kid livin' in fear,
    Then he went one day that he won't play that,
    The Dealer co' fucked him up, and ended it with a pimp slap,
    He's fuckin' him up everyday, and he always has a set up,
    One day he beat up Shorty's girl, and then he had his boy wet up,
    My Shorty went crazy, and you know he lost his mind,
    One day he left wit some large bills, and then he came back with a nine,
    My Shorty left one night, and caught him on the DL,
    He blasted his ass twenty times, and then he took his steel,
    Now my Shorty's changed, cause his ass is always packin',
    You never get him heated, cause he always starts cappin',
    My Shorty runs around, now livin' like a gangsta,
    Fuck messin' with them drugs, he'll just cap ya, and he'll gank ya,
    My Shorty ain't the only one, a victim of the syndrome,
    The Hood Life mentality, it's hits you in ya dome,
    Now you need power if you wanna squash beef,
    And have to spell g-u-n if you want relief,
    Gots problems from the dealers, gots problems from the crews,
    Get your hands on the steel, and gots nothin' to lose,
    (Yo) it's only the beginnin', cause my Shorty ain't done,
    It's part of hood life, son..
    Lawz unda da gun...

<u>Chorus</u>:

Lawz Unda da Gun

<u>Verse 2</u>

Shorty's runnin' around actin' so crazy, that you'd think that he was Satan,
    Shorty's own girl knows, cause she's tryin' to change him,
    But the nigga won't listen, so his ass is still wild,
    And he's even fuckin' wit cops, and he's still just a child,

Once was a genius, and now he's just crazy,
His dreams of bein' a scholar are now just really hazy,
He used to be a coolie, and take care of his girl,
Takin' care of his moms, the nicest kid in the world,
Now his ass is known, the baddest kid you ever saw,
A li'l nigga wit a gun who can even quick draw,
He lived large for a few, then one day he had beef,
My Shorty started buckin', and then he took it to the streets,
He's runnin' through the buildin's, and he's still lettin' off,
Still chasin' them beefers just to show he ain't soft,
He ran into one building to catch the last beefer,
And he had a massive shootout, one that he ain't figure,
Shorty started runnin', and then he saw him face-to-face,
Money was too close, and scared, so he capped him with no haste,
He fell to his knees, his gun in hand, and still scared,
He came too close to death, even farther than he dared,
Shorty's girl came out, and then she caught him by surprised,
He turned, and shot her by reflex, and then he'd seen her die,
Shorty ran over to her, and then he started screamin',
He held her in his arms, with her blood still streamin',
Shorty shot his girl, and his unknown son,
And now he's locked down....
Lawz unda da gun...
<u>Chorus</u>
Lawz Unda da Gun
© 1993-1994

FOR THE CENSORS

I try to kick the truth to the youth, you say its radical lies,
    And then you wonder why it's *you* that I despise,
    You think I'm just a nigga from the street, you think I'm just a vote..?
    Well, think again before I punch you in the throat (*yo*)
    You call me angry, and talk shit when I raise my fist,
    You wanna censor something, motherfucker...censor this,
    Can't wear my clothes, parlay my ways, or how I'm spending my days,
    I try to organize, and see how it pays,
    (*Nope*) It don't work, it's just getting' dissed, and kissin' up,
    These fake ass sellouts and preachers that they be hypin' up,
    I can't stand authority, so you claimin' that I'm disrespectful,
    No more of the bullshit, I'm just givin' you a mouthful,
    Ya feelin' threatened when confronted wit your crimes,
    And then you start to flinch, hearin' line after line,
    You try to lie your way out, say that was back in the days,
    That the oppression is over, that all debts are repaid,
    (*BULLSHIT!*) You're full of shit, I can't speak of what ya do to me,
    But you can always crucify if we practice unity,
    Can't say what I want, you try to silence my verbal cries,
    (*Full of lies*) And then you lie on me, right in front of my eyes,
    These double standards gotta cease right this minute,
    Since you're the one who started this shit, I'll fuckin' finish,
    (*Yeah*), You think you're bad, you really think you're muy malo,
    So come get in my face, I'll kick your ass wit my zapatos,
    For the masses that have missed, and also felt dissed,
    You wanna censor somethin'...? Motherfucker, Censor this!

Chorus: (4X)

You wanna censor somethin'...motherfucker, censor this

Verse 2

If I dress Hip Hop, then you call me a thug,
But then if I were a white boy, it'd be a cultural bug,
Then if I'm in the streets, I can't roll wit my crew,

Cause you say I'm out there doin' crimes, doin' shit I don't do,
I'm always getting judged, but it's wrong if I do it,
Yo, tell me how is that? Now that's real fuckin' stupid,
I hate oppression, and I hate all you wannabes,
You always tryin' to copy me, and then you wanna fuck wit me,
I don't think so, I'm livin' instilled realness,
You always talkin' ying yang, talkin' bout shit you don't deal wit,
You little suckas say that you're livin' PC,
(*Nah*) Yo ass ain't foolin' nobody, nah...you ain't foolin' me,
You teach me lies in school, and then you say that it's the truth,
But when I challenge what I'm taught, you try to give me the boot,
Just cause I'm from the streets, ya wanna call me a hoodrat,
But if I call you a hipster bitch, then you say I can't do that,
It's my mouth, and I'm gonna speak my mind,
You fear my intellect, that of the rebellious kind,
I try to represent, and I try to live righteous,
But you claim its militance, and then you try to divide us,
You say that I'm too young, and that I don't know any better,
But then when *you* fuck up, I can't use that against ya,
I'm tired of your mouth, don't try to treat me like a chump,
Cause I'll smack your dumb ass silly, fuckin' bitch ass punk,
It ain't over, this ain't that last that you heard of this,
You wanna censor something...? Motherfucker, Censor this!
<u>**Chorus**</u>: (4X)
You wanna censor something...motherfucker, censor this
<u>**Verse 3**</u>
And for my one love...they say I'm out here makin' babies,
Well, I say that you can bite me, and I hope that you catch rabies,
I make a little loot, so now you say I'm dealin' drugs,
Man, your makin' me laugh, you know that's soundin' really bugged,
You're talkin' down to me, and then you're treatin' me like dirt,
You know you're so full of shit, that you make my fuckin' colon hurt,
These fucked up politicians, and these move fakin' preachers,
Also these sellout parents, and these backstabbin' teachers,
Amigo, please...bring some common sense to the battle,

I'm gonna take you out, and then I'll brand you just like cattle,
Don't sleep on me, son, you gotta know this is my time,
I'll rock you back and forth like you was livin' on a fault line,
Know how I roll, fuck all that bein' a role model,
I cypher as a teacher cause I was never one to follow,
Kickin' my own thoughts, not down wit popular opinion,
I always had my own mind, was never anyone's minion,
be beamin' like the sun, or be rainin' on parades,
Cause when I start to kick knowledge, like an Uzi, you gets sprayed,
So get outta my face, cause this the last time I warn ya,
Cause you know I'll smack you harder than a sock full of quarters,
For the brothers who resist, them backstabbin' bitch,
You wanna censor something...? Motherfucker, Censor this!
<u>Chorus</u>: (4X)
You wanna censor something...mother fucker, censor this
© 1992-1993

PHUNKEE HONDURAN'S FLOW

P-H-U-N-K-double E
    And at the end put Honduran, and you know that's me,
    Now here's a phunkee introduction of how nice I am,
    (*Hey!*) I make illiterates speed read through Sam I Am,
    I gotta kick it for mis niños, how their people vivimos,
    When I start to preach La Raza Unidos, (*Uh!*)
    I earned the right to be called the Phunkee Honduran,
    Cause it's the audience I gets learnin', and other emcees that I'm burnin',
    Encyclopedias ain't no comparison,
    I kickin' out so much knowledge, it's them paper scholars that I'm embarrassin',
    The self-knowledge that I'm kickin' in on the level,
    Cause I'm lifting up my people, and I'm scaring them chinga wetos,
    Goddamn right, call me a Buffalo Soldier,
    Cause we always saved your ass in battle, in every war, over and over...
    (*Punk mutherfucka*) All your prejudice lies are disappearin',
    And our self-knowledge is droppin' bombs just like the Tuskegee Airmen,
    I'm still learnin' the pen's mightier that the sword,
    But we still need the help of Brown Berets and Young Lords,
    My artifacts cannot be beaten by false attacks,
    But step to me, I'll go down fighting just like the Caribs and the Arawaks,
    The many weapons I have at hand to beat ya,
    Amaze you with Obeah, or maybe use some Santería,
    (*Ya fucking heathen*) Ya can't stand it, ya startin' to hate it,
    No longer can you dominate, your ass is overrated,
    You ain't en vogue son, and never will be,
    Your time has come, get fucking lost you Silly Willy,
    I've found my mission, and I'm stayin' mad focused,
    I'll make you crippled worse than even multiple sclerosis,
    -It's hopeless- A higher intelligence can't be defeated,
    And payback's a bitch, 400 years worth of cheatin',
    From the Black, Brown, Red, and even then some,

And eventually, you'll get poisoned by the many deadly venoms,
Tick tock, tick tock...ya time is going,
I'll probably say good riddance by the time I'm finished flowin',
To all you suckas and haters that's tryin' to harm me..?
You're more of a little bitch than that Transformer Star Scream,
Tired of fightin' and beefin', and all that nonsense,
I'll stick to elevating consciousness, and other mental concepts,
To all my peoples and brothers that's down to love me,
Who sit there cypherin' change, along with other ethnic studies,
Back in the dayz, reminiscin' from way back,
To all my souljahrs battlin' to stay on the right track,
From the creator of Spanish People In Control,
It's time to bid good riddance to the Phunkee Honduran's Flow

[Alternate verse ending]
I'm full of intellect and mad respect, I'm here to catch wreck,
Can't step to me, you know I won't let you protect ya neck,
The K-A-S is never frivolous, never ridiculous,
Ya battle me, and you come out odoriferous,
You can't combat my mental presence, ya feelin' my essence,
I'll overpower you with an intelligent sentence,
-Defenseless- You'll never outwit my mental prowess,
Ya wanna talk shit, then back down...? That's pure cowardice,
I'll educate you on the facts I know are real,
And try to pass on that knowledge, try to keep you on the straight deal,
Don't need a movement, I can be positive by myself,
Instead of runnin' with a crew that puts ideals on the shelf,
Ya wanna blow my spot, ya really think ya mad callous..?
I'll blow your shit up brighter that the Aurora Borealis,
I'm not a bully, not a sucka...no, I ain't a punk,
I'm not a wannabe that's crystal clear is a chump,
From the creator of Spanish People In Control,
Just down to let you hear the Phunkee Honduran's Flow

<u>Chorus</u>:
On the culture tip, give me respect for the props I'm earnin'
(*Why..?*) Cause I'm the Phunkee Honduran
© 1994

PART II:
Heart of a Lover

TO MY QUEEN (MY DEAREST MONICA)

To my Dearest Monica...

I cannot tell you the severity of the hold that you have on me,

Whenever I look into your eyes, it makes me want to scream inside,

The sweetness of your voice, the sexiness of your shape,

It takes all that I have to control myself around you...

You are so sweet and sexy, but also very refined,

A lot of class, with a little bit of edge,

Perfect, in my eyes...

To my Dearest Monica...

If I could ask but one thing of you; a single, solitary request...

All that I ask, is for one night...

From sunset, to sunrise,

Just one single, solitary night, to experience you, and please you...

To please you like none other ever has before,

To fulfill your wish, your every desire,

Sensual pleasure at its supremacy...

To my Dearest Monica...

My angel, my fantasy...to the one that excites me so,

First, I would lie you on your stomach, and give you a gentle massage,

Accented with kisses all along your lovely, shapely frame,

Teasing your backside and buttocks...

Then, I would lie you on your back, viewing you in your full beauty,

First...exploring your sweet, sweet lips and mouth,

And again, accenting your body with passionate kisses,

Hitting every erogenous zone that I know that exists on your body...

To my Dearest Monica...

Hearing your soft cries, excited by your moans,

With you wanting more, I gratefully oblige...

Kissing you all over your chest, and down to your stomach,

Tickling your navel, and still descending lower...

First, tasting you all over your thighs, first inner, then outer...

And then...and then...

Pleasuring your lower level with oral delight,

Pleasing you until you can take no more...

And the best is yet to come...

To my Dearest Monica...

To make you feel treasured is what I seek,

Yes, you are wanted and desired,

To be able to, first, pleasure you...a necessity...

To then finally be inside of you, and experience your sensual power,

All of this, while a soundtrack of love songs fills the background,

Reminding us of each and every part of this treasured moment...

It is to you, my Dearest Monica, that I wish this upon...

Could this be us, for real...?

© 2000

Dedicated to Monica Alvarenga

MY FANTASY

"I came upon the desired abode, as per your request,

Upon opening the door, I am greeted by two rows of lighted candles forging a path into the darkness, leading me to My Fantasy...

I enter, following the lit path, leading me this way and that,

And the path finally leads me to this mysterious, yet attracting door...

I open the door, and peer inside,

And a delightful sight greets my eyes...

The room is illuminated by the candlelight that fills it, and at its center..is My Fantasy,

Lying in a tub full of milk, looking at me with love in her eyes, and other intentions besides...

With a smile and a wink, she beckons me over with her finger,

and of course, I gratefully oblige...

I shed my wardrobe, take her hand, and step inside the tub, settling myself next to her,

Starting off...I gently massage her shoulders, all in the while, nibbling...

First, on her earlobe...

Then, down the nape of her neck...

She then turns to me, and we taste each others lips, feeling their fullness, tasting each others sweetness,

With both of us exhibiting the passionate heat and eroticism of the moment...

As we look into each others eyes, we enter into a new level of emotional consciousness,

As our bodies intertwine with each other, as only soul mates and lovers do...

We put all of our passion, all of our love, into this natural act,

Growing closer and closer to each other with each and every movement,

Then, finally, upon releasing all of our impassioned energy, our lovemaking reaches its climax...

We lie back, safely and caringly in each others arms,

At this point in time, as I've always told you before, I tell you with all of my heart that, I love you...

But, there are a few more words that I would like to tell you, someday soon…
It's goes along the lines of, "I do"…
That…is My Fantasy."
© 2000

WHAT WOULD IT BE LIKE?

" What Would It Be Like...

To hold your hands in mine, and look into your eyes,
　　And see what you are feeling, from the bottom of your heart,
　　To the depths of your soul...
　　What Would It be Like...
　　To be held in each others arms, as the melodic sounds of a romantic ballad
fills the atmosphere around us...
　　What Would It Be Like...
　　To walk out in public with you, hand in hand,
　　And feeling the ravenous envy of others, because they're not in my position....
　　What Would It Be Like...
　　To tell you those three very special little words for the first time,
　　And seeing your reaction, because you know that I really mean them...
　　What Would It Be Like....
　　Damn, I wish I could tell you..."
© 1998

A JEWEL IN MY LIFE (I & II)

Part I

"You are a Jewel in my Life,
Shining like a beacon in the darkness,
Living up to your name, being both precious and rare...
Giving me the utmost pleasure,
I cherish you for what you give me,
Fore you are not a symbol of status to me,
In my eyes...you are a true prize...
Though I may not be able to have you in my life,
You will forever be in my heart,
My sacred, precious Chrystal,
You truly are...a Jewel in My Life,
© 2000

Part II

To The Jewel in My Life,
To you who is constantly in my thoughts,
My precious gem, always lingering in my mind,
I can't stop thinking about you...
Fore if you are my sickness, then let there be no cure for me,
Your sensual silhouette, how sweet you smell,
The softness of your touch, the way that you make me feel,
How I wish that you were mine, and mine alone...
One can dream, can't he...?
If only you knew...
How much I want to please you,
How much I want to pleasure you,
How much I want to be in your heart, as you are in mine,
I hope that it's not too much to ask...
It is only because you are so precious,
Tu siempre tienes mi corazon,
Te quiero, mami, te amo mucho, mami...
© 2000

SPITTIN' LYRICS N WAXIN' POETIC

Dedicated to Chrystal

LOVE LETTER

"To my dearest...
To the one who reigns supreme over my heart,
To you who dominates my thoughts,
I just wanted to drop you a line, to let you know what's on my mind,
Wanting to let you know exactly how I feel about you...
I wish to be with you, and only you,
I wish to give you my heart and soul,
I wish to give you all of my affections,
I'm willing to give you all of me, with no regrets, or reservations...
I want you to have me, there is no doubt in my mind,
None other shall come into my heart,
None other shall fill my vision,
It is you, and only you that I seek,
Fore you are my one and only true Queen,
And as my Queen, I shall be many things to you...
A King, that rules by your side, helping to pick you up when you are down, or feeling weak,
A Champion, who always fights for your honor from those who would dare to hurt you, or disrespect you,
Or, a humble Worshiper, who will always love you unconditionally during times, both good and bad...
I am all of this to you, and you are so much more to me,
The joy that I feel when I am able to make you happy, and see you smile,
The way that you inspire me to do the things I do for you,
The way those three little words swim through my mind whenever I am with you,
And I shall say them to you, sometime soon...
All of this is for you, and the best is yet to come,
That is, of course, if you'll continue to have me,
Signed...One who is yours, truly..."
© 2000

COURTSHIP

"To you, who art thine own sweet personal Juliet,

To you, who art so smart, sweet, sexy, sophisticated, and oh so beautiful...

I've become completely mesmerized by your chocolate, chocolate essence,

My heart always beating, my soul always tingling, whenever I am in your presence,

My mind is constantly preoccupied with thoughts of you,

The urge I have to show you my affections for you in every way possible is overpowering,

Looking into your mystic eyes, becoming enraptured by your natural beauty,

Your exquisite figure, your full lips, and sweet smile, exciting and inviting me...

I want to invite you into my heart and soul, giving you full possession,

Also wanting to show you how much you mean to me in every pleasurable way,

You see...I once wrote a poem call "To My Queen",

And it's only with you that I would want to re-enact that scene,

Caressing you, pleasing you, and loving you deservedly so...

To have you walk around in an effervescent glow and permanent smile,

And, of course...always doing the little things, just to make you happy,

A poetic verse here...some roses there...writing you letters ever so often...

I choose to do all of this just to let you know how much you mean to me,

These words are spoken for no other reason than to have you in my life,

No ulterior motives, no self-serving purpose...

I want to be able to look into your eyes, and know what you're thinking and feeling,

To hold you up when you're feeling weak, to cheer you up when you're feeling blue,

Questions for you my sweet...

May I hold your hand in public...?

May I show you public displays of affection...?

Do you enjoy being serenaded by love songs...?

Do you like it when those little words are spoken to you...?

You see, I do have credentials in holding this type of position in your life,
My last employer did not appreciate what I had to offer,
But, I know that this time, with you, things will be different
Let us see, shall we?
© 1998

ODE TO LISA

"What's the first thing that comes to mind when I am thinking of you?

Is it affection, is it infatuation? Is it as close as I'll get to honestly feeling love?

Or, could it be lust in disguise?

Well...maybe, just a little, somewhere in the back of my mind.

Then again, maybe it's all of the above.

But alas, they are genuine feelings that I have for you.

Be they be innocent, be they be deep....

be they be ulterior motive, be they be part of a master plan...

They stand honest and true for you.

'Fore with your presence beckons the memory of many adored love songs, past and present.

What can I say...you just have that affect on me.

The feeling of a valiant knight championing for his princess comes to mind.

For the sake of true, unadulterated romance...shall we make this dream come true?"

©) 1998

Dedicated to Lisa Gomez

ADWOA (I, II, & III)

<u>**Part I**</u>

"To you, I extend my heart, my soul, and my mind,

Wanting you to own a little part of me.

This is a gift that I've chosen to share with very few...

And, with great pleasure, you are an honoree.

Why you, you ask?

'Fore it is the coolness of your aura, the sweetness of your heart,

The aire of sophistication that you carry yourself with...

All of these qualities that you possess magnetize my attention,

Drawing me into your sphere, with you becoming that which I desire.

I have visions of sharing myself with you in the most intimate fashion,

Letting you know that what I feel for you, is real.

It is my greatest hope to be accepted into your world,

Becoming a part of your life.

Bless me with your presence, bless me by showing in return that which was given to you...

A place in the heart."

©) 2001

<u>**Part II**</u>

"The sweetness of your aura excites my mood so,

The coolness of your character commands my full attention that I willfully give.

Your voice sends pleasurable sensations that orbit my vessel...

Those eyes, that smile...both having a complete hold on me.

One simple truth.....I've got a Jones for you.

I have many dreams for many days and nights,

With you in the starring role in this mental cinema...

The many ways I wish to court you, and gain your heart,

Always ending with me expressing how I feel about you in the ultimate fashion,

Forever dreaming of asking for your permission to make love to you.

And, with permission granted, pleasing you as you should always be pleased.

I wish nothing more than to be admitted into your queendom,
Worshiping you, and loving you with all that I have.
You will forever exist in my heart of hearts,
'Fore that is all that I ask in return.
Blessed be me, I grant this to thee."
©) 2001

Part III

"The deepest levels of infatuation infest my soul,
Drawing you into my mind and heart in a constant flow.
Your silhouette possesses my mind, a never departing vision,
Accompanied by your mystic eyes, your lovely smile, and sweet voice.
Why must you have this hold on me, sweet one?
Furthermore, why do I like it so?
Wishing to express to you everything that I feel in my heart,
Wanting you to know just how much I'm feeling you,
How much you move me, how much you motivate me...
How much I want to include you in my world.
To touch you in the right spots, to feel your warmth next to mine,
To do all that I can to please you, and make you happy.
I am pleased just to have my life graced by your presence.
You can truly be the one that got away...
These genuine, heartfelt emotions are my parting gift to you,
A humble worshipers' offering to his Nubian Queen.
They are yours to keep, Sweet one.
You shall always reign over my heart."
©) 2001
Dedicated to Adwoa Ansah

SONIA'S SONG

"Would've, should've, could've...

All of these phrases enter into my mind whenever I think of you,

Remembering how I let you pass me by without ever addressing how I felt about you.

I cannot give a definitive answer as to why I kept my interest in you bottled up inside.

From the first time I saw you, standing by the elevators one winter day...

Our eyes linked us together, in more ways than one.

As I passed you by, we exchanged smiles with one another,

And I knew right then, that I was smitten by you.

I would always look forward to seeing your lovely form, greeting you often.

But, alas, for some foolish reason, I never pursued you beyond that point.

I have spent many nights, and many days, lost in thoughts about you...

How better to get to know you, how I could gain your heart,

How to properly show you that what I feel for you, is genuine and real.

There were moments when I gained the boldness to approach,

But, time was not on my side, with preoccupations filling your mind.

Alas, I shouldn't have let anything keep me from gaining that which I desire.

To look into those brown eyes of yours, to be graced by your honey chocolate essence,

Constantly watching your muscle-toned temple pass me by...

You make a man want to scream, "Oh...my...god!"

Perhaps it was for the best that it never had been, you and I,

'Fore my tamed character may not have been enough to satisfy you.

I at least would have liked the opportunity to try and see.

Now...I'll never know."

©) 2001

Dedicated to Sonia Pugh

SMILEY

A smile, one that emanates throughout the darkness,
One that can guide you to peace and serenity,
The calming affect that a smile can have on others,
Easily easing all tensions, and providing warmth at your coldest hour,
The power that it has to subdue some, and to energize others,
The power that it has to insure order in a chaotic world,
From the time of our first encounter, that power has been bestowed unto
you...
I've witnessed it's effect on others, and it's effect on me,
The light behind your smile is bright and true,
To see you time, and time again with the same smile on each day,
I want to know what it is that makes you feel this way...
Hoping to see your smile's uplifting presence just one more time...
What is it about your smile that intrigues me so, you ask...?
Its warmth, its innocence, its honesty, its illuminance,
Then again, a smile is only as bright and pure as the person who wears it...
A smile reflects what is in a person's heart,
So, may your smile shine brightly,
Illuminating even the darkest days, and darkest hours,
And, may my smiles one day return the favor to you,
signed, and sealed, with a kiss...
(Mwah)
© 2001
Dedicated to Leigh Gomez

LUST

"You are so sexy beyond definition.

Your sex appeal goes unmatched by any other...

I stand mesmerized every time that I see you.

I am addicted to your beauty,

Needing to see you time, and time again.

If you are my sickness, then let there be no cure for me...

I've wanted to be with you ever since I first saw you.

Your grace, your elegance, your corporeal silhouette that is the definition of true beauty...

The eroticism that you give off entices me more and more.

It fuels my desire for you almost to the point of insanity...

I want to be with you!

I want to experience you at every possible level...

I want to experience you intimately, spiritually, emotionally, physically, and also sexually...

I want more than just instant pleasure, more than just satisfaction.

I want to bond with you, even if it's only for one time.

You are not an object to be possessed, but an experience waiting to be shared...

Do I have your permission?"

© 1999

LETTER FROM MY HEART

"In your moment of sadness, I feel your sadness and pain.

When you smile, my day is brightened, like the moonlight lighting the darkness,

Or the sunlight illuminating the day...

When you are troubled, I feel compelled to solve whatever ills your mind and soul.

I want to always be there for you, and always protect you from any and all harm.

I love it when I get to hear the sound of your voice,

Even if you only talk to me for a few minutes, I am left satisfied.

I want to do so much for you...yet I don't know how to go about it.

I want to take my time with you, yet I want you to have all of me, now.

I want to tell you so much how I feel, yet I don't want to overwhelm you, and scare you away.

I want to be your lover, but I am willing to be your friend for right now,

'Fore we don't know what the future holds for us.

To be there for you...a necessity.

Plus, I *want* to be there for you.

I want you to be touched by my words because, for me, they have meaning.

The honor and integrity behind my words are the truth for you to see.

Never to wish intentional harm unto you, never to deceive you...

I want to be able to express my heart to you, and for you to know that I mean it.

There are certain things that I want to say, that I want to do...

All in the name of making you happy.

Let me be the sacred water that washes your troubles away...

Let me be that charm that always brings you good luck...

Let me be the one that will make you happy, always.

It's a wish that I hope will come true.

These feelings of mine needed to be expressed to you,

For they were hard to contain inside of me.

My greatest wish is that you'll have me.

If not...then it is my greatest pleasure to have gotten to know you, and experience you in my life.

I want many things in this life...

To be your friend, to be your lover....to be the love of your life,

If the future would be so kind to me...

I hope that you will always treasure my words,

Because I really mean them...and they're only for you.

Signed....from my heart, to you."

©) 2004

THE ART OF LOVING YOU

"The Art of Loving You...
The main ingredients are the following,
Unconditional love, honesty, and understanding.
Throw in a dash of emotion and affection, some dedication,
And a lot of devotion.
Mix all of these ingredients together with an open heart and soul,
Until you get a warmth that has never been felt before.
This is a recipe that I would make every waking moment for you.
It would be part of every meal, always an opening appetizer,
Served up nice and warm, only for you.
I love you so much, I hope you know.
You would be served this special meal every day, every meal,
Whether as breakfast in bed, or late night snack.
I would hand feed you this meal, watching you as you sensually taste the morsels offered to you,
Licking your delectable, juicy lips, of the sweet sauce of love and life.
After helping you to feast, I would gently massage your feet, pampering you as best I can.
I would slowly move up to your thighs, gently and softly rubbing your legs, letting you feel the warmth of my hands, hitting every erogenous zone on your lower half.
I would then touch you in your private place, feeling how warm and wet you are,
Adding the warmth of my tongue to this adventure, tasting you in your essence.
I would feast on you for a while, feeling your wetness, tasting your sweetness,
Hoping to hear your moans and cries, signals of your pleasure and happiness.
I would feast on you, until you could take no more, but still wanting me to continue to pleasure you,
I would move further north, tickling your navel, tasting your all over your body,
Tickling your nipples, tasting the whole of your breasts.

Your neck would be my next target, tasting you all over,

Moving on to your succulent lips, as juicy and moist as they are,

Tasting all of your love for me.

We would then bond with each other, making love as only two soul mates are capable of,

Enjoying each other for as long as we can, until infinity.

Our passionate bonding would be sealed with a kiss, and us professing our love for each other,

Sharing an ultimate experience that no others are capable of equaling.

Loving you is an art form, a supreme skill to be mastered,

'Fore it is the only way to truly please, and honor you.

I wish nothing more than to make you happy, and to fulfill your every desire.

That is why I cherish....the Art of Loving You."

©) 2004

ABOUT LAST NIGHT

"About last night...

I couldn't stop smiling, a permanent grin etched on my face all night long.

I was honored to have been able to spend time with you, graced by your presence,

Getting the opportunity to bask in your beauty.

I was touched by your poetic words, returning the affection that I continue to show you,

Feeling so overjoyed, feeling so honored that you expressed your love for me.

I loved how you touched me, how you made me feel,

Allowing me to live out one of my fantasies with you, making love to you by candlelight,

With incense burning, and soft melodic music playing in the background.

To be able to share myself with you, filled me with the greatest sense of joy,

Also being able to hear you express your love for me in return, a blessed event indeed.

The rest of my night was spent thinking of only you, and how happy you made me,

Hoping to get to see and hear from you the next day.

My love for you grows more and more, enhanced every time we are together,

Wishing that you would never leave my side.

Our night was ended with a good night kiss,

A perfect ending to a perfect night.

I do wish that you could have stayed the night, to be able to make love to you all night long,

But, alas...there is always next time.

I thank you for being with me, I thank you for loving me,

Hoping that we will always continue to have nights like this one.

You mean so much to me, as I hope I mean so much to you,

Praying to the spirits that we shall always be.

This is for you, my love, my way to thank you endlessly,

...For last night.

I love you."

BONDING WITH YOU

"Bonding with you was everything I ever dreamed it would be.

To be so close to you, feel so close to you, to become one with you...

To be able to share each other time and again; the ultimate in pleasure...

I wanted to love you more and more, never leaving your side,

Continuing to bond with, and share each other all through the night.

We were able to connect with each other on a higher level,

Pleasing each other, being able to become in tuned with each others spirit.

I've never wanted anyone before, the way that I want you.

Never wanting to let you go, wanting to continue to please you in every which way,

Wanting to make you happy all night long, if need be.

As I was rubbing your body down with cocoa butter, I never felt so wanted, so desired before.

Hoping to tantalize your senses, stimulate your erogenous zones, I rubbed you so gently, so passionately,

I wanted you to feel the passion that I have for you through my fingertips.

You felt so warm, so smooth, as your body shined in the dim light of the room,

The surrounding music enhancing the beloved mood, as only love songs can.

I felt so much joy, so much pleasure being with you, that very moment,

Stimulated beyond all comprehension to continue to be with you.

You had me so aroused, so taken by you,

I would have pleased you until my last breath.

I thank you for sharing yourself with me, becoming more open, us becoming closer,

Bonding with each other, the way our souls were meant to.

You give me so much joy and happiness, so much pleasure,

I hope that I can fully return all of the pleasure and happiness that you have always given me.

You are the sunshine of my life, you will always be the one.

You are the apple of my eye, what drives me to do what I can to take care of you, and aid you in your times of need.

I never want to let you go, I want to hold you in my arms forever,

Always making you happy, knowing that you love me, as I love you.

Thank you for letting my fantasies come true, Thank you for living them with me,

Thank you for loving me as you do.

I wish to bond with you until the end of time, always together.

May we always be in each others lives; living, loving, caring, sharing, giving...

I'm glad to be bonding with you, for you are the only one I would ever want to bond with.

To you, my love....for always.

I love you."

©) 2004

MORE THAN A CRUSH

"I must admit...I have a big crush on you.

Actually...it's more than a crush.

When I'm not with you, I am saddened by your absence,

When we are together, I wish for time to stand still forever, so that we can always enjoy these moments together.

I *do* become a little jealous when other men enter into your sphere,

Only because I wish that I was in their position.

You are constantly on my mind, and in my thoughts...

How better to make you happy,

How better to excite and entice you,

How to let you know that my affections for you are genuine,

How better to gain your heart and confidence.

I lay down at night, dreaming of ways to enter into your heart,

I rise, hoping to get the chance to see you that very day.

You're highly intoxicating, and I am addicted to you.

The only treatment....acceptance into your sphere.

This poetic communique is designed only for you,

My thoughts and feelings for you being presented in the best way I know how.

You excite me so when I hear the sound of your voice,

My heart beats a different rhythm when you enter my plane of vision.

My feelings of fondness for you grows by the day.

I hope that you feel the same way...

May you always cherish these feelings that I have for you,

May your feelings for me grow, in return.

I would love nothing more than to be in your heart, as you are in mine.

I know, I know...strong sentiments to be made, when our time together has not been very long.

Alas, I know what is inside, and I know that it is true.

I just needed to let you know...I have a big crush on you.

Actually...it's more than a crush...."

©) 2004

SO OPEN

"You've got me so open....

I feel like I can tell you anything, and everything about me.

My darkest secrets, my deepest desires, my inner most thoughts...

My past and deepest thoughts are at your disposal.

I feel that I can let myself be open, and vulnerable to you,

Never to be judged, never to be cast aside.

How do you get me to feel this way?

I look deep into your eyes, and feel so...free.

I feel that I need not hide anything from you, fully exposing myself.

It's scary, but thrilling and liberating at the same time.

Being totally honest with you, letting down my guard,

Just openly baring my soul to you.

With you, I feel that I need not hide from you, concealing my true inner self,

Showing you, not only my best qualities, but also my flaws and weaknesses...

My insecurity, my self doubt,

My varying levels of self confidence, my pride,

My infamous temper, my habitual internalization of my frustrations,

Being selfless to a fault, my fear of eternal loneliness...

I want you to know all of this, and to not be afraid of me, or my love for you.

I want to be honest and truthful with you, always.

Admittedly, being so open can be frightening...

But, I feel that you are a worthy person to instill my trust in.

Quite easily, I can become emotionally attached,

Making it easier for me to fall in love with someone.

Because of how you stimulate me, how you inspire my heart and mind,

I find myself falling hard for you.

I pray this feeling of euphoria never ceases, existing for all our time together.

I can't believe that you got me so open, like this.

But...I like it. I like it a lot."

© 2004

LIFTED SPIRITS

"On bleakest day, you persevere,

When your heart has been broken, you persevere,

When the chips are down, and life seems against you...again, you persevere.

I truly admire you for your strength of will.

It inspires me so, leading me to believe that if you can persevere through dire situations,

Then I can overcome mine, as minor as they are.

I wish nothing more, than to be there for you in your time of need,

And to give you the utmost support that I am capable of giving you,

Helping you to get through whatever ails your mood, and life.

I truly wish that I can do more for you at this time,

But, because of my own predicament, I'll have to stick to giving you all of my love and support.

Wanting the best for you, to be able to aid you, protect you, in your times of need,

A shoulder to lean on, a fountain to give you added strength,

I just want to be there for you.

Though these times are trying, and the circumstances seem mean and unnecessary,

You will arise, and overcome.

My ultimate best will be given unto you, to help you to overcome, doing my part for you,

Making sure that you come out of all of this, with your head held high and triumphant.

Your strength of will makes me love you, more and more,

Proud to be in your presence, proud to be a part of your life.

I will go above and beyond to keep your spirits lifted, making sure that they never falter.

This is a promise that I make to you, giving you my word as a gentleman, and as one who loves you so.

You inspire me to greatness, to do the best that I can to help you, and make you happy.

May your spirits be lifted by my words, and the deepness of my love for you.
You will never be alone, and forever be in my heart.
You will achieve, and succeed, my love.
I love you, so."
©) 2004

TO MY DEAREST YANA

To my dearest Yana...
I love everything about you...
Your lips, your smile, your laughter and humor,
Your sultry and curvy chocolate form, whether covered or not,
Your beautiful hair, in its natural essence, no matter its color,
How you make me feel when we are together, your laughter and open mind,
How you never judge me, or look your nose down on me for what I believe,
For loving the little gifts that I give you, both literary and cultural,
For always being so supportive of me, whether silent or vocal cheerleader,
To being open and inviting to the cultural jewels that I gift to you,
To my dearest Yana...
I thank you for your friendship, for considering me to be a dear and true friend,
For the trust that you give me to be so open and forthcoming in our conversations,
To supporting me in my career to express myself in the literary field,
For the countless moments of pleasure that we shared together, etched into my mind,
Forever a classic cinema treasure trove of bliss and erotic excitement,
Sharing competition with no other...
To my dearest Yana...
I hurt when you hurt...feel sadness when you feel sad,
Cry inside when you are struggling, being that shoulder that you lean on,
Empathizing with you, when the negativity that is penetrating your soul weighs you down,
Hoping to be that avenging angel that decimates all that ails you,
To be that protector and provider that you so deserve...
To be the lucky one that earns your love and heart,
To win your hand in blissful matrimony,
And bear a few more little ones into this world, enriching both of our lives...
For making me want to be a better man,

To be that positive male figure in your life, that both you and your little one can look up to,

To be that man that you will be proud of, to want to have in your life,

For you to be proud to announce publicly that, "Yes...he is *mine*!"...

To my dearest Yana...

I love you more than anything, of that I hope you know,

I love to hear your voice, to look into your face, to be in your presence,

To be near you, to wrap myself around you, and give you my love unconditionally,

To see you grow spiritually and intellectually, becoming more mature,

To embrace your essence of womanhood, improving and perfecting yourself,

Becoming that queen and empress that you were meant to bc...

To my dearest Yana...

May you reach all of the pinnacles that you were meant to reach,

Just know that I love you, and support you,

And will always be here when you need me,

Doing all that I can to assist you...financially, physically, or in spirit,

Always having your back, being your rock,

Giving and returning to you, the unconditional love that you so deserve,

Having solidified your place in my heart...

To my dearest Yana...

I really love you; I just wanted you to know that.

Te amo mucho, mi amor...

:-*

© 2015

Dedicated to Tatayana "Yana" Gee

THE DEPTHS OF MY HEART

If only you knew....
    When we first met, I wasn't expecting it to happen,
    I didn't even have the slightest hint...
    But then, the more that I got to see you, and know you more,
    The more I realized, how deeply I cared for you,
    Straight, no chaser...
    I never knew how important you would eventually become to me,
    Realizing just how much you mean to me,
    Just how much I want you, and need you in my life...
    Wishing that I could do more for you, and your little one,
    Being able to be that provider, that rock, that support that you need,
    To be that true man that you so deserve to have in your life,
    That shining example of what a strong brother really is, and can be...
    I wish that I could tell you just how much I do truly love you,
    How much I want to be in your life on a more intimate level,
    To love you, honor you, and cherish you, until our days beyond this plane...
    But...that's not something that you want at this point,
    And I must respect your wishes, no matter how much I want to be with you...
    To let you know just how much I love you, and want to be with you,
    To share my life with you, for you to be a very important part of it,
    To bear more powerful seeds with you, with two loving parents,
    A proud example of what a strong Black family should be...
    To be a shining example of strong Black love between a man and woman,
    How an empress should truly be treated; revered and worshiped,
    Fully loved, honored, treasured, and respected by her mate...
    I would love for this to be us,
    But...not until you're ready for it, and truly want this from me...
    But, until that time when you are ready, when this is what you want,
    I will patiently wait, controlling my love for you,
    Keeping it in reserve, until that cherished time...
    If you only knew of the depths of my heart, how much I feel for you,
    The multiple levels of my love for you, How much I want to give it to you,

You might reconsider the wait...
Of course, you need to be ready and willing,
For you are trying to get yourself right, straighten your life out,
Do what is needed and necessary to take of yourself, and your little one,
I can truly and deeply respect that...
So, I will patiently wait, helping when and where I can,
Holding all of this good loving in reserve,
Ready to unleash it in its full capacity, unrestricted for you,
Ready to take it to intimate levels never seen before,
Only for you, and you alone...
I dearly love you, truly and deeply,
Hoping to be yours, to share our lives together,
To let you see the depths of my heart,
And how deep it is for you.
© 2015

UNRESTRICTED

I would love to tell you that I love you,

Uninhibited and unrestricted, not afraid of the consequences thereafter,

Not fearing any type of rejection on your part, making you uncomfortable...

I would love to be with you normally, as a man and woman should,

Out in public, hand in hand, your arm wrapped around mine,

Publicly being able to display as much affection as I feel for you,

Proud to have you by my side, and in my life...

I would love to propose to you, and figure out the little things about our union,

Where to hold it, who to invite, our song to dance to,

Will I relocate to you, or you and your little one to me,

Will you and your little one carry my name, or hyphenate,

How many brothers and sisters should we give her, ;-)...?

I would love to explore our spirituality together,

Reaching higher heights, expanding our spiritual awareness,

Getting more in-tuned with nature, closer to The Creator,

Balancing our chakras, embracing our true essence,

Becoming that ultimate man and wombmyn that we were meant to be...

I would love to explore the world with you,

Truly knowing our history and heritage, embracing our true culture,

Unplugging from this society, and knowing the truth for ourselves,

Being able to pass that on to our little ones, letting them truly know who they really are, And NOT what this wicked society tells them, and trains them to believe...

I wish to give you my full love, unrestricted, unfiltered,

All of it, fully and completely, in total,

And love you like you so deserve....

:-*

© 2015

ABOUT THE AUTHOR

KEVIN ALBERTO SABIO is an author and activist. He is the youngest of three children of Honduran Garifuna immigrant parents, and born and raised in Brooklyn, NY. He attended Newbury College in Brookline, MA as a Mass Communications major, and graduated from Southern Connecticut State University in New Haven, CT with a Bachelor's of Science in Video Production. He is the author of five books: *"Raise Your Brown Black Fist: The Political Shouts of an Angry Afro Latino"* (Authorhouse, 2010), *"Raise Your Brown Black Fist 2: MORE Political Shouts of an Angry Afro Latino"* (Outskirts Press, 2011), *"In My Lifetime: Funny Stories of Life Experiences"* (Outskirts Press, 2014); and the fiction novels *"The Chronicles of the Black Fist (A Superhero Novel)"* (CreateSpace, 2015), and *"Demure Nights"* (CreateSpace, 2015). This is his first book of poetry.

He is the founder/creator of the **Universal Africana Literary Arts Movement & Expo**; an independent networking group, and grassroots event aimed at highlighting and promoting the endeavors of African descended peoples in the various fields and industry of literature; from authorship, to publishing, to distribution. He is also the founder/creator of **The Consortium of Afro Latino Communities**; an independent grassroots event aimed at highlighting, promoting, and exposing the African roots and heritage of Latino people through films, literature & book signings, and panel discussions.

You can find the author on social media sites such as G+, Facebook, LinkedIn, and Twitter. You can also follow his blog at www.brownblackfistchronicles.blogspot.com[1].

---

1.   http://www.brownblackfistchronicles.blogspot.com/